Subtle Poesy

AF362582

OrangeBooks Publication

Smriti Nagar, Bhilai, Chhattisgarh - 490020

Website: **www.orangebooks.in**

First Edition, 2022

ISBN: 978-93-5621-075-2

Words tugged at heartstrings

Subtle Poesy

Dr Upma A. Sharma

OrangeBooks Publication

www.orangebooks.in

My husband Ajit Sharma for believing in me, my son Kartikeya Sharma who has been a constant inspiration, my mother Sumitra Gupta for her everlasting affection, my Dad Prof. Anand Kumar Gupta who lit a spirit of determination in me, my brother Vasu Aggarwal for his unending support and my sister Jyoti Aggarwal for her soulful love.

I am also grateful to my family, friends and colleagues for encouraging me at every juncture of life so that could I never put my pen down.

About The Author

Dr. Upma Aggarwal Sharma is doctor by profession and leads the Community healthcare programme of India's leading Pharmaceutical company under CSR. She did her MBBS from Govt Medical College Patiala and Post-graduation in Health and family welfare management from National Institute of Health and family welfare, New Delhi.

Poetry is a passion for her & she has been writing for last four decades. She believes that penning is the only way to satiate appetite for words, words that are born out of mind rustles, rhyme with the heartbeats and are a way to serenity.

About The Book

This poetry book is an anthology of 102 poems that came straight from heart. True emotions as if immersed in ink to express some joyous moments and lot more melancholic times. Many words unsaid that remained tugged at heartstrings, having streamed their way into the pages of this book.

Readers will be able to get deep into the heart of the poet and pull strings to release the melody & feel the subtlety of sentiments.

Index

Caves

Truth as tiny drops of water
hangs onto roofs,
Waiting to nurture thoughts
creeping on dark floors,
Strange mind caves...

Till flash of bright sunlight
traverses through,
For negativity to vanish
and sets dormant ideas aglow,
Strange mind caves...

Memories

Alongside the serene river stream,
I lie calm as my little dog hops by;
As morning Sun shines bright,
flowers bloom in most vibrant colours;
Giggling to the tune of soothing wind,
joyous butterflies subtly flutter.

While I recall those rosy days of youth,
and cherish echoes of once irresistible laughter.

Faith

Faith like a magnet
attracts and embraces,
Rises as an early sun
touches acme of noon,
Soothes as a cool breeze
to soul's serenity,
Blooms as vibrant flowers
an emblem of Spring.

Faith if defied
bleeds as malignant ulcer,
Whips the very soul
and squeezes the heart,
Nibbles ruthlessly
to later discard,
Moves in a dry desert
as hope chases mirage.

What The Eye Sees Heart Cannot Forget

A descending sun
and orange of dusk,
Reflects in the river
with fading twilight,
Is the world conquered
or is it an aura of defeat ?

When moving water
doesn't change direction,
When greens on banks
still dance with breeze,
Birds return to nests
Rests the horizon,
Every morning sun
rises in the east.

Pull up veils of night sky
let fears fade in moonlight,
If no stars twinkle,
let glitter those fireflies,
Hold tight the reins
as mind horses run fast,
Treasure in heart
the unforgettable beauty,
The dreamy eyes see
and soul cherishes.

Paintbrush

The creator while painting the universe,
Added brilliance, with vivid colours
to Mother Nature;

Yellow sun became orange at the twilight,
Seven colours of rainbow, an ethereal delight;
Various notes of green to trees in abundance,
Snowflakes on tops shimmered silvery
and extra white;

Shades of blue in changing sky and deep ocean,
Colourful birds, marines and fishes
getting illumination;
Cherries and strawberries, cardinal red
and crimson,
Roses and tulips, red, pink, yellow,
lavender and salmon;

Glistening mountains became golden at sunset,
Vibrant colours sing melody from His trumpet;
But an eye to appreciate His picturesque,
Else for a pondering mind to wisely imagine;

When I saw the painting, it was mostly ashen grey,
To my wonder why could he not script a better play;
He then assured and gave me better eyes,
Eyes of the mind stronger than those
for colours and dyes !

In The Desert

Like a barren flute
punched and airless,
Amidst sand dunes
and dusky plaits,
Where no roses bloom
only cacti prick,
Lonesome, desolate,
as emotions daunt,
Tears dried up
I writhe in ache.

Yearning for...
A melody,
A rain,
A smile,
A little red rose...
that he might bring,
an utmost utopia.

Masks

All masks are finally gone;

Enough of hand wash
and tangy sanitizers,
Those drapings on nose and mouth.

Months of work from home
late morning wake ups,
Now rise from your comfort couch.

Free from ailment fears
and restricted wanderings,
Let's get ready with the travel pouch.

Covid era is about to end
with jabs mark surpassed,
Having witnessed ugliness
as pretty looking faces unmasked;

Doctors left in blue
as mankind shed its hue,
Like incessant rains
when patients kept pouring,

Warriors had lives at stake
as Covid came roaring,
Even cremated those dead,
when their very own tread;
Two years of cold blood
and finally some warmth;

Many precious lives lost
as tears flooded young homes,
Humanity lost its colors
camouflaged several times,
Left to die in streets
as leaves of autumn crushed,
Healed elderly abandoned
by their own blood ;

A Mother's wait is over
as remorse drowns in tears;

But for the masks of diplomacy
an unending greed for the land,
To prove its mettle
and invoke fears of wars,
Will those cruel minds
ever embrace subtlety,
And give up the swathes;

For the time has come
to breathe in some fresh air !

I Miss You Here

*Sudden blush on face
as my sobbing heartbeats throb,
How I missed you all these days;
Yearnings set ablaze
to melt in your warm embrace,
Tears burn my rosy red cheeks.*

On My Return From London

Happiness of meeting dears
and then the pain of parting;
My longings fail to give up
to the things most heartening;

Back to memory lane...

When Sun rose with tender smiles
and opening of those little eyes;
As giggles marked end of the day
with everyone draped in clay;

Those were the days...

When we were purely at will
appetite of the chimney and grill;
Holidaying whole day through
with melody of lyrics imbued;

Those were the days...

Then thick books kept us awake
getting up in the mornings late;
So many questions, how, when and why?
till curious mind rested to tunes of lullaby;

Those were the days...

Time has flown, memories remain
over the years wasn't tough terrain;
Colourful person turned to drip
solitude hits hard like a whip;

These are the days ....

My soul stays there
as I halfheartedly return,
Putting smile on the face
while those irresistible tears burn.

The Rose

Simmering on a low constant flame,
Lacking visible steam and smoke;
The red blood became more deep in color,
Is the rose of my heart!

Adding onto day after day,
The fragrance became more intense;
Sans to lose essence and sheen,
Is the rose of my heart!

Perpetual Longings to stay close to you,
The gap became lengthened so far;
Ineffectual to lose charm and craze,
Is the rosé of my heart!

Someday I will attain you absolute ,
Incompetent to predict those golden moments;
The time surely will favour it bloom,
The Rose of my heart!

Dripping Emotions End

When dripping emotions end up in stare,
all churned up humour, fuming breaths of flair,
Subtle shreds of heart foresee no mend,
a waning smile these tender pieces pretend;

Shuddered by endless tides of strife,
evanesced the faintest melody of my life,
Plethora of thoughts and broken threads,
rests tranquil the soul, at deepest beds;

Expressions of ache, in vivid colours carved,
no twinkle in eyes, my looks are scarred.

Muse On The Loose

Boundless rumination...
is like
meandering abyssal,
as plethora
of thoughts deluges;

Unable to
find direction,
Diving endlessly,
Till a poem
born at last
merely by default.

A Sonnet In The Wind

A musical wind blows at my door,
Low frequency soft soothing tone;
Euphony that mesmerises down the floor,
A musical wind blows at my door.

I am at peace with my soul,
Alpine harmonious delightful tone;
Enchantment that lives down the floor,
A musical wind blows at my door.

The wind blows swift and jazzy I go,
Recapture the dreams that constantly flow;
Ephemeral delight that exacerbates,
The wind blows swift and jazzy I go.

All the detriments ameliorate,
The wind blows swift and jazzy I go !

Music To My Soul

As plucking of strings
rhymes with my heart,
Water of the wild springs
dances from its very start;

The iota of droplets
allures as luminous pearls,
Yen my buoyant dulcets
to tame all luscious hurls.

Friendship

Setting a hopeless day aglow,
Adding sparkles to a dark night,
Emotions and trust nurtured to grow;
As tranquil silvery pearls of moonlight,
Friendship sets the most dismal face bright.

Trapped In My Own Thoughts

Years have passed by as I still writhe in pain,
Grief nibbles slowly of my deep inside;
Hunting joy in pool of negative thoughts,
succumb to my own false perceptions.

Melody seems to lose to dissonance,
Altruism read as animosity;
Nurturer confounded as assassin,
Creator misconstrued nefarious.

Waiting to be rescued in murky night,
Yet not wanting to trust visibly kind;
Thrown further in centre of the whirlpool,
I swirl fast to rest on tranquil seabed.

Gratitude

Perpetual fragrance of life sojourns in air,
As golden glitz of sun swigs despair;

Nature endows its riches on us to cherish,
His boundless bounties will never perish;

A tranquil soul that plucks strings of kindness,
will relinquish soreness of brutish heartless;

Let magnificent aurora of dawn unfold,
and emotions of gratitude rise manifold.

Tears

Tears shed on the grave
Unable to secure calm,
As wild tides of sea
the intense sentiment floods,
All fervors end in despair.

Two Pairs Of Shoes

As solitude
gripped me tight,
Heart ached in anguish
and I gasped for sigh...
Everything lay still.

But then I could
rise and shine,
In tender blush of dawn
as I woke up to find...
Two pairs of shoes
at my door.

Love In Barren Land

I sow my love in barren land
as tears water
blood manures
no buds bloom
inhumanity crawls;

Dust shadows the bright sky
dark clouds veil
cries the blue
and masked moonlight
hatred rips my soul;

There comes no twilight
no new sun rises
lost in absolute black
wailing through night
to erratic sleep's embrace;

I sow my love in barren land
and wait and wait
eyes end up in dryness
heartbeats regress
nothing to anticipate ...

Spring flowers

Artemisia bear the colourful foliage
Bluebells carpet a magical sight
Coreopsis and cherries blossom
Daffodils are seen in jovial mood
Eranthis buds as the snow melts,
Forsythia screams it's spring time,
Grape hyacinths trumpet arrival
Hellebore shows surprising resilience,
Irises have a charmed goodness,
Japanese anemones pop up in cheer,
Kangaroo paws giggle,
Lilacs give sweeter fragrance
Moss phlox jewels open alongside tulips
Narcissuses dance in joy,
Oriental lilies add colour and drama

Pansy prefers being cool,
Quietude of poppy charms
Redbud feasts for the eyes,
Snowdrop anemone fragrances fortune,
Time for hearty Asiatic lily to hail,
Unfolding beauty of Orchid,
Virginia bluebells and viburnum
Witch hazel adds touch of yellow
X factors in birds of paradise,
Yellow trillium adds a true zing
Zinnia gives lasting affection and goodness.

Hiding

It was fun I couldn't resist,
An adventurous trip by office guys,
And so I lied to my wife!

She would not try and understand,
Monotony at workplace we face in our life,
And so I lied to my wife !

Imagine I can't come out of the hiding,
Since to Malaysia by hijacked MIG I flied,
Friends and home, scared of the plight,
Just as I lied to my wife !

Beauty And Diversity

With a thousand and one diversities
defining beauty sounds moronic,

Deep blue eyes and glossy skin
that patently are a lover's whim,
Ornate the wrapped dry emotions
and a stone cold heart sometimes,

While an awful look cannot ensconce
the warmth and brimming allegiance
of mind and thoughts that never fail to entice.

Beyond The Breakers

There lived a princess,
more charming than anyone;
Living in a giant castle,
hidden in dense forest.

Days rose with radiant sunbeams,
gnomes played little games;
Fairies chased in the garden,
Horses tapped in unison.

Twilight dusk unveiled her beauty,
as the mighty Prince would return;
Serene moonlight could not spell,
The magic beyond the breakers.

The peaceful kingdom,
to be sung on the big screen;
Rested tranquil through the nights,
darkness melting to the aurora of dawns !

My family

cultivated, groomed
as I cherish ways of life
my roots, family...

imprinted on mind
moments of togetherness
lived in ecstasy...

some of the sorrows
unsaid, embed deep in heart,
unfolded in time...

some bitter conflicts
walking down memory lane
slowly skip aside...

through all thick and thin
counting on those silent tears
family stands by...

A Dead Man

Golu was 3 then, on our way to school,
he gave me directions as I drove,
saw one man lying motionless in blood pool,
he could easily make out the man was dead.

"What's dead I can now tell you mom" he said.
I was curious to know his thoughts.
He told me that as the tyre goes flat when it deflates
since air is gone, the body will lie still
when all the blood is gone.
Appreciating thoughtful concepts
of my bright little kid,
I told him that there was more for us to be dead,
and the air in mention was actually the parting soul.

As the tyres go flat, he now firmly believes
that the soul must have left.

Even The Angels Wept

As I walked amidst stars
to find my glitter fade into their twinkle,
With my dears I was at war
loneliness reflected in my wrinkles,
Few smiles in darkness if life could sprinkle...

Heyday of life and many promises unkept,
To knocks of heaven, even the Angels wept.

Future

Appreciate, revel in
purest dreams of the unborn,
Savour your present
till veils of soul be left torn,
Future never is forlorn.

Soul Consciousness

Conscience without a body
no brain, no thoughts,
no heart, no emotions,
no grief, no joy,
no smile, no tears,
how can consciousness be?

Soul, an electric stimulus
to enlighten the brain,
to make us ponder,
Body else a pile of dust,
will not glow
if soul fails to nurture,

Many souls that surround
put on thinking caps,
That chisel and sharpen
to discover logic of life,
A spirit of positivity...

To be engraved on souls
as consciousness...
For generations to reinvent
the purpose
Be it followed or not ?

(Inspiration- Why is it necessary that soul
consciousness be achieved while in the physical
body?
Is this the purpose of our souls being encased in the
physical body?)

Colourful Art

secrets of nature
that glass art substantiates ~~
vibrant florals dance

My Son My Pride

A moment of ecstasy
of being a mother,
A reverie of life gratified.

I saw a glitter as you opened
your tiny eyes,
My very existence glorified.

Your charming brio
and unsaid words,
Graced us with your fervor.

You smiled, sat, stood, walked
and ran around,
Your little hands, tender kisses
and sweet rhymes.

Your first day to school,
your excitement,
Adored by teachers,
grew to a vivacious being.

As you unveil your intellect,
rise towards achievement of your goals,
Stand alpine with persuation,
blessed with no dearth,
we all beamed with pride.

How could I let slip of my memory,
Joyous days when we resembled,
And few sad days of fight
when tears rolled down the eyes.
A congruous relationship we had
for all those golden eighteen years.

Myriad thoughts occupy my mind,
I dream of the day when
you reach to the absolute.

God bless you dear son
with His immensity !
May you stand sovereign,
embellished with perseverance !

Promises

Your promises that I had all trust in
lay quiet as logs of unbreathing woods,
Till wantings of my soul rose as fierce storms
to impute life into the forgotten,
Today you walk with me in moonlit night
as longings lay absolutely tranquil.

hevey

Rain O' Rain

As I wait for rain
that quenches thirst of the dry soil,
Longing for petrichor rises
as breaths anticipate new life,
Magical raindrops
flow in veins of Gods...
Armistice to soul's content,
an essence for the ebbing,
Heavenly earthy incense
no worldly aroma can match ...
Drenched in icicle drizzles
I hang onto year after year,
waiting for His eternal scent.

One Hundred Years Of Solitude

As solitude of rich sunset
embraces my intense pain
and takes me onto glory,
Freedom comes as prized beget,
intoxicates into gain
self searches turn Ivory,
logic consumes my deep anguish!

Once Upon A Time

Once upon a time,
there lived kindest of souls;
In the trunk of a tree,
In a palace built within.

Illuminated the tree stood tall,
its fluorescence dripping in darkness;
As the sky pulled a black sheet,
sun calmly descended down the hills.

Thoughts rode on swift horses,
and travelled through the night sky;
Souls afloat amongst twinkling stars,
bathed in serene moonlit night.

With bagful of glittering gifts,
Fairies with a magic wand;
Granted all wishes and turned dreams true,
To unveil mysteries, heavens beyond.

As the morning sun rose,
desires returned and rested;
Embed deep in the hearts,
Once upon a time.

Emotional Deluge

When deities set a divine retribution,
How civilisations can breathe a sigh,
Forget not Noah's gesture to build an arc,
So all species could recreate new world,
Such strong is human craving for life....

Anticipating His turn to keep a promise,
Rainbow as a sign may absolutely suffice,
As emotions deluge the subtle heart,
He sends logic to rescue us afloat,
those seven vibrant colours paint us bright....

As My Sister Played

Eager to teach, my sister
played musical amalgamation,
as my sweet Ashika learnt
with great concentration,
Guiding her little hands,
putting strings to vibration,
Jyoti could lay for her
a very strong foundation,
as we anticipate her grow
with finest reverberation.

Tiranga

Saffron to renounce
dharma spins in peaceful white ~~
soil gives green for life

The Indian flag- Tiranga- meaning Tricolour
(has three horizontal bars of colours saffron, white
and green embossed in the middle with a Navy blue
Ashok Chakra (wheel) Saffron or orange denotes
valour and selflessness, renunciation and
absolution of ego).

White for honesty, purity and peace, symbolic of
light to guide our conduct on path of truth.

Green for faith, fertility and prosperity, represents
life and happiness by virtue of Earth and soil on
which all life is dependant.

In centre is blue coloured wheel with 24 spokes
represents truth and dharma, wheel denotes motion
that keeps us moving forward and represents
dynamism of peaceful change.

Heavenly Himachal

Snow clad hills with sun's silver shine,
Whitened by moonlight like crest of waves,
Tree covered folds in the mountains,
Are like a gigantic crumpled velvet rug,
Soft and supple twigs hanging intertwined,

Turbulent rivers flow flawless through the heart,
Rains drizzle and seep deep into bones,
A gaze through a mist of fluffy clouds,
Smoky night sky and stars await twinkle,
Chilly breeze that preserves the smile,

God in every bit can be seen alive,
Alongside the serpentine path as you thrive,
Serenity to soul view from every angle grants,
Heavenly abode leaving never would you want,
Feel melody in heart and song in the air !

* Himachal is a state in north of India.

Passion That Enchants

Trust my love
Trust my passion
Passion in hearts
Passion to souls
Souls that crave
Souls that dance
Dance to the tune
Dance through night
Night so long
Night so bright
Bright as stars
Bright as sun
Sun that sets
Sun that shines
Shines every day
Shines each life
Life that blooms
Life that giggles
Giggles like mad
Giggles when sad
Sad in fears
Sad in tears
Tears in eyes

Tears of parting
Parting uncalled for
Parting quite sudden
Sudden are doubts
Sudden come clouds
Clouds soft white
Clouds take flight
Flight in skies
Flight of thoughts
Thoughts of Valentine
Thoughts of love
Love that lasts
Love that blasts
Blasts of emotions
Blasts of notions
Notions so true
Notions heartfelt
Heartfelt till core
Heartfelt evermore
Evermore for a while
Evermore sweet smile
Smile that graces
Smile that enchants
Enchants to content
Enchants till tranquility
Content
Tranquility...

Dolor Ebbs Valor

As I sob in deep midnight darkness,
bleeding tears of his betrayal make me drown...

Lose way in whirlpool of incessant thoughts,
I leap to cut through and through,
Subtle desires breathe last...

Ecstatic beats can't help muffle down,
rhyming hearts no more send melody,
some broken beads of diffused parody,
Plucked strings snuff my clown...

The bruises on soul
silently traipse abysmal,
blackness I embrace
ferrying the albatross,
Bane of dolor ebbs valor.

Carrying His Baggage

Sparkling bride keen to bloom apace,
was rattled bitterly by groom's embrace,
Who shrouded her glitz in taunts,
burdening with baggage of dos and don'ts;

The tender heart bruised savvy,
bounty tears to eyes were heavy,
Perishing youth, pondering in past,
magical words lay frozen aghast;

Point came where tolerance ceased,
Pie in the sky, a new dawn squeezed;

Putting off the unwanted, bust the bag,
freedom and life, her two wishful tags,
I the bride, my liberated bubbly soul,
am onto conquering of realistic goals !

Home

*Hues of twilight melt
to embrace tranquil darkness,
Only to find a solace
after wandering is put to harness;
Moments back home when
very air soothes the restless soul,
Every morning croak of raven
is a feel of heaven.*

Ebony

As denied passion in memories stings,
while yearnings churn up a still crazy heart,
Stains of hatred on purest mind it brings,
for life, subtle soul remains deeply scarred,
Vivid thoughts twinkle and then drift apart.

No stopping to tears that flow in despair,
Condemned be time, engulfing all the flair,
Trust and love obsessed into agony,
absolute darkness would defy the fair,
unless unveil these clouds of ebony !

A Telepathy

I feel your touch
as breeze caresses,
first ray of sunlight
you send to enlighten,
No distance
can undo my longing,
I dance to the tune
of your magnetic vibes...

"Inspiration-
To telepathy of your love, my heart wildly flutters".

Triad In 7 Beats

Tears as serene morning dew
Hang onto subtle thought strings,
Lavalliere decors my soul.

What Might You Find There

Subtle desires, crushed and squeezed,
Static sanguine, those collapsing beats;

If kindness could creep very inside,
Till depth of tears and smoky eyes;

His name engraved in ink of passion,
Amidst bruises of betrayal and aggression;

Beneath broken ribs, pieces of zest,
Shaken restless soul, longing to rest;

Every tranquil breath, find him there
Just to rub my bleeding wounds bare.

Walking With Your Eyes Closed

Kids roam in the streets
as schools cry for more seats,
Many sleep in hunger
while food in the bin creeps.

Can you lend a helping hand,
rather than walk with eyes closed ?

Youth smitten by money
losing morals to iniquities,
Drenched in luxuries
a living masquerade.

Can you catechize ethics
or still walk with eyes closed ?

Abusing nature for greed
exploiting feeble and fleece,
Plundering water and soil
looting air and oil.

Can you fix up this and end
or blindness would you pretend ?

Proving valour in bouts of spar,
to quench this thirst in name of war,
Sitting on throne conquered in ashes,
crowned in Bloodshed.

Would you aggrandize and greet?
Treasure time will else fleet,
And stop walking with your eyes closed.

Victim Or Victor

My bubbly being sought an end,
the day he lay tranquil, no pretend;

Dark clouds swiftly veiled my rainbow,
took away the charm and brilliant glow;

The world came crashing, a bruised soul,
as if life with him was the only goal;

Depressed and dejected I wished to die,
as time ditched with that grieving sigh;

Till a heavenly heart came to my rescue,
made me feel I had still left some due;

Struggling amidst wild sea and all strife,
finally I was through all negatives of life;

Would have been victim, turned victor,
cherishing fruits of His worldly splendour.

Bees

Tiny souls buzzing
and humming,
Swaying with
air waves afloat,

As rich colourful
florets beguile,
Fragrance in breeze
antenna senses,

A gratifying feast
of nectar regales,
While no endeavour
to touch the sky,

Hoists the pollen
in nescience,
Benevolence of
nature redefined,

Twilight of dusk
they return to hive,
Mustering honey
is a bee's delight !

Vibgyor Bows

Splashes of rain dare
amidst thunder of dark clouds ~~
seven colours shine

Unrequited Love

Incessant blooms of adoration
craved to be prized,
As treasures of my passion
were utterly defied,
Musical notes tugged at heartstrings
the harmony denied.

Cupid was out of arrows,
Unrequited love...

What melody could not teach
the pain did,
While silence didn't hurt
the words did,
Grieved a heart when I lost the one
that was never mine.

As Passion On Face Glows

The igneous lava flows
within the tender heart
as passion on face glows,

Parting rips the soul apart
black when replaces light
within the tender heart,

Despair brumes the bright
tears cascade chubby cheeks
black when replaces light,

Emotions manumit as creeks
Ecstasy airs the memory lane
tears cascade chubby cheeks,

Not letting sweetness wane
thumping beats send the gush,
Ecstasy airs the memory lane,

Soothes a tranquil brush
The igneous lava flows
thumping beats send the gush,
as passion on face glows.

New Year

New year begins as
a new chapter to be written afresh,
Make sure it is worth
reading time and again,
Let the goodness
of earlier pages troll an impetus;
So the buoyant spirits
breathe in zeal and inner faith,
May successes accrue
as we all rise in absolute grace!

The Day After Christmas

Night of celebrations
when merges into daylight,
Christmas carols send
everlasting musical delight,
Wrig of mistletoe
where souls have clung tight,

The day after Christmas
comes with festiv echoes,
Joys boomerang,
ecstasy perpetuates,
Till Santa wears all red
and wakes us up again,

A power nap for some
that danced through night,
While for others
A fuming Boxing Day !

Chasing A Rainbow

Craving for respite in torrid weather,
Some rain that could tranquil drought;
Memorising festal times revered together,
Wondrous moments of numero uno brought.

Nothing could abridge my deep anguish,
How long and hard I must have tried;
Sadness or depression to distinguish,
Euphoric apparently I although pried.

Hidden beneath murky veils of dolor,
Tugged at heartstrings, the twinge;
Await wisdom spring in brilliant colour,
As I stand on a thin tender fringe.

How long will relentless waiting end,
Many tiring years have passed by;
How far made up joys can I pretend,
When life has lost its being of why.

Will go off the clouds, emotions burst?
Will lightening set dark mind aglow?
Will thunder crack the negativity first?
Anon, I might be chasing a rainbow.

Oh So Beautiful

Orange twilight hues
crushing sound of autumn leaves ~~
tranquil sunset chirp

The End Of The Road

As the twilight of sunset
elopes into blackness,
Nature blows its trumpet
spreads veils of darkness,

Fragrance of soft breeze
diffuses into vastness,
Chirps and all shrieks
end in deep quietness,

My passionate heart weeps
embraces an absolute zero,
I lie amongst those creeps
soul sinks in aqua deeps,

My blood turns to frost
I return to heavenly abode,
Standing I am, entirely lost
as if at the end of the road.

I Be An Owl

You rest at night as I hoot,
   hanging onto the wires
As you sleep in your homes.

Then label me as a symbol
   of misfortune and misery,
Forgetting the misdeeds you do.

I could see and turn around
yet the cheats and cruelties,
In your mind were invisible.

I thought you would love
and care and nurture us all,
With gift of God to mankind.

What's In A Name

Lost in words was my passionate heart,
As rising sea would spit me back to the start;

Every sunrise unfolded a new horizon,
Arrows pricked me deep to shed poison,

Rested all my desires as I pretended dead,
My soul lay tranquil in deep seabed;

In an amazing world full of similes,
Honey drips to the buzz of bees;

It's all fortune, hard work and fame,
What's there anyways in the name?

Just A Little Bit Of Sugar

After a day's hard work
tranquil in twilight's halt,
Blood burns in success
and sweat tastes of salt,

Just a little bit of sugar
is all what you want.

Tough times in life
when soaked in strife,
Sun shimmers at its peak
no rain of relief in sight,

*Just a little bit of sigh
is all that you want.*

*Dark veils of gloom
in bouts of depression,
When cloud the mind sky
and zero down expression,*

*Just a little bit of light
is all what you want.*

Fiery Sand Of A Hot Sun

Cool
Smoky
Ruckus minds,
Sedate torrid
Sands.

You Don't See What I Do

You don't see what I do,
Just b'coz you don't want to...

The vibrant beauty of mind esplanade,
Jubilance afloat in pleasant breeze,
Emotions pristine simmered in aubade,

You don't see what I do,
pretend to be a mannequin...

While heart beats in absolute rhyme,
radiate rosy blush to red cheeks,
When passion could nurture no mime,

You don't see what I do,
altruistic if you be, I doubt...

Muffled sound of cold heartbeats,
sluggish blood dragging in veins and
Frigid perpetual stare on face fleets,

Is what you have become,
Insensitive and fancy-free.

Losing Self

I lose myself
In many colours of my child's laughter
In soft caress of those candid smiles
In sleepless nights of innocent cries,

I lose myself
On busy roads that once led to school
On weekends usually long awaited
On festivals and family celebrations,

I lose myself
As I pass by the shopping malls
As I wait outside of cinema halls
As I queue up for Nando's n chillies,

I lose myself
To relive memories etched in time.

Snapshots

Sitting by calm riverside, adjusting the aperture,
As mind attests the perfect landscape to capture;

Taking few small leaps, not to leave a nuance,
He is fast ready to click a string in temerity;

Be it anything, a marrow or a barren,
His shoots whisper countless historic tales;

A flower's subtle bloom, or an old man's humility,
Nothing escapes his intense proclivity;

He awes by seizing sea's fierce turbulence,
Butterfly's flutter, through hues of sunlight;

Images of rivulets dancing to nature's melodic raga,
These picturesque snapshots will sing the saga !

Mend Thyself

When skin creases and silver colours the plait,
Nest empties, then starts that endless wait;
Better be your own best friend,
Part with that dull trend;
Stay happy,
Mend;
Dress snappy,
Defy ageing, blend;
Youthful times don't ever end,
Let sweet melodies reverberate;
When skin creases and silver colours the plait.

Yearn To Learn

On hot summer day...
Follow the mirage,
Or the corsage.

Try that once...
Dance to tunes,
Along sand dunes.

When you reach the peak...
Climb the hill,
And just chill.

History comes alive...
Must visit Castle,
Without any hassle.

Decide on joyrides...
Enjoy camel ride,
Watch great stride.

Yearn to learn...
If mind deserts,
Then it hurts.

Cloudburst

*With dark clouds
of incessant gloom set to burst,
Clarity shines first;*

*Subtle winds caress
as fragrance goes in air,
Imagine the flair;*

*Melody unveils in
a sparrow's soft chirp,
Dances every twerp;*

*Overflowing emotions
set turbulence,
Ocean's pure essence;*

*Only to quench thirst,
The heart at its worst,
With dark clouds
of incessant gloom set to burst.*

Better At Hiding

Imbued in vast ocean of grief,
as emotions dig deep;
Heart pounces on my soul,
I bid adieu to a great dad;
Tears scroll down in miffed sleep,
lunar tides go tranquil.

Wayra Lantern

Quiver of light goes
with fast storm of murky night;
lantern loses on its weight.
Could hear some soft whispers
but he wasn't anywhere in sight.

Depression

Once so bubbly and cheerful
how purposeless now seems the life,
Fingers fail on the holes of flute
air no more blows in rhyme;

Even if hundreds of Suns combine
can't get me a little sunshine,
Thousands of stars twinkle
heart sees only white of moonlight;

Sitting within forewalls of closed room
I await something bright however minuscule,
In that darkness of biting cold
anticipate some soothes of warmth;

Like a weightless tender feather
for days that could remain afloat in air;
I too seem to be hanging onto this life
although no reason to such a strife;

Soothing breeze doesn't embrace
soft whispers unheard,
Colourful paints cease to charm
flowers as if have no essence;

Unlike an old volcano
having used up all the brimstone,
I don't even boil or simmer
despite all the fire underneath.

To My Teacher

You imbued ideas
into our subtle minds,
and nurtured them sagely;

You made us ponder
so that we choose the righteous,
and walk through our lives
with confidence and pride;

You my dear teacher
are the one to shape our future,
It was all your hard work
that with ease we can rise and shine.

Autumn Afterglow

Amazed at autumn's splendour
maple leaves rest in grandeur,
It's a stunning morning twilight
compliments the garden vividly bright,
Yellow and brown, winds sway
Crushing sound of crispy walkway,
I sit on bench after brisk walk
as friends gather for little talk,
Gracefully the preceding exfoliate
so abreast the boscage rejuvenate,
Green mellowed into colours of fall
Picturesque beauty takes the stall,
Outsets in daylight saving tempo,
Mesmerising autumn afterglow.

Destitute Must Thrive

Contrary to the forlorn attitude,
Thrive for the bliss of solitude,
The vulnerable gets incapacitated,
Keep spark of optimism inside alive !

Helpless gets sturdy, will not mentally die,
Heaps of benevolence, keeps living a lie,
Struggles till the woes get precipitated,
Spark of hope always burns alive !

Languishing tribulations seem incumbent,
A muscular man declared impotent,
Munificent heart asthenic and debilitated,
Spark of hope still stays alive !

Miseries are vaporous, only if comprehend,
Toreador if be, will turn vilipend,
Embrace potvaliancy, rather remain paralysed,
Must keep spark of hope alive !

A Daydream

Treasured lyrics of life in my hard bound collection,
Melodious rhyming notes of heart
and fingers unwind,
An age old piano, still and all, sings to perfection,
As I unfold pages to a daydream of heroic mankind,
Plagiarise every budding music of soul and mind !

Diamond Dust, Devil

Diamonds in the rough,
Make the dust fly,
Dust and ashes
The devil comes alive !

Earth in its deep inside
Is full of arrogance
Erupting volcanoes
Devastating beauty,
Blind to the
Observer's delight !

The storms, tornadoes
Never stay calm
Join the darker side,
Moonlight sprinkles
Diamond dust in
Night's dark waters !

Under deep oceans
Lava bubbles out,
Red crater at midriff,
Rainbow colours to
The whirlpool surrounds,
The devil to pay !

Zeus O great Lord !
The thunderer!
Give the devil his due,
The devil takes the hindmost !!

Rock My World

Far away from harsh reality,
Where monotony of life prevails,
Let me live in the dreamiest world;
Every moment to jump with joy,
Folding and unfolding in middle air !

Sitting on the back of giant terrapin,
Dancing to the tunes back and forth,
Rhyming with the drifting sea tides;
Unending rungs of ladder are visible,
Hierarchy of desires, climb up the sky !

Twined strings that take me to heavens,
Where Freedom of body, freedom of spirit,
Get an essence maybe fiction and fantasy;
Truth may be a stranger, fiction is truer,
Be it an illusion, must Rock my world !

Red Moon

Happiest of times, sometimes we have to repent,
Although Ascending lunar a fortunate omen,
Yet breathtaking tides of full moon,
can cause torrent;
Sad moments thrust utmost emotions,
can be a boon,
Add up to unsurpassed beauty
of the eclipsed Red Moon!

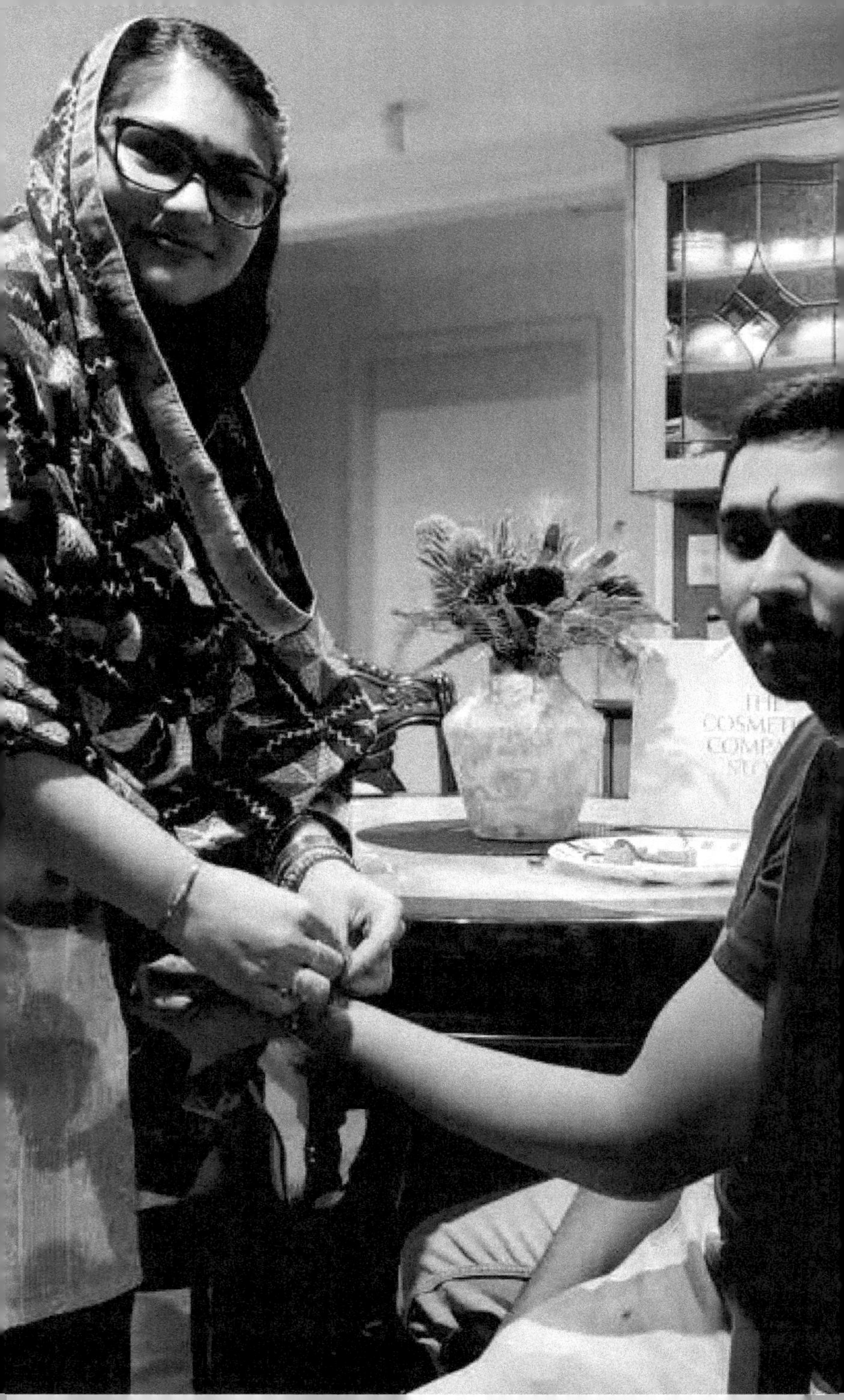

Threads Of Rakhi

Threads of Rakhi entwined in love,
Connote a sister's love for her brother,

Love that got obscured in busy life,
Distance progressed as we adored our families,

But only seemingly parted,
Souls still one and a single thought,

Born of one mother,
lived together for years
Celebrated, faught, annoyed,
conciliated and understood each other,

Endeavoured on all topics,
Lived by each other in all thick and thin,

Childhood days are not just memories,
But to cherish and a reason to live,

Some family values,
expressed by subtler gestures,
And immersed Into these fragrances,
are tender strings of Rakhi.

Sturdy Cowboys

Sturdy cowboys
Evolved as heroes,
Well built, stout featured,
Wooden attire
Arched hats, spiky shoes,
Tough looks as is life !

Farmhouse mornings,
Saddle the stallion,
Solid hoofs sound,
Get into the saddle
For a day's ride,
Horse around or about !

Leading the herd
Get on high horse,
Appear out of woods
Clouds of dust follow,
Awaken devils
Legendary heroes !

Scripture Alchemy

Speaking volumes in the youth literary,
An ordinary pen of a humble grey mind,
Shimmers, be it favourable or to the contrary;
Smooth flowing thoughts, of its own single kind,
Now mature enough with exclusives to grind !

No One Lives His Life

Born with a silver spoon in mouth,
Brought up royal, tamed in discipline,
Childhood joys were living in a dream,
Every stage of my grappling life,
Was a huge blow to my very being.

An always ought to prove myself situation,
Books and hard work made me scream,
Sublime artist inside me died and cried,
Smile of success masked my inside fight,
Dancing to the tunes of the master planner,
He thwarted even the best of my rhymes;

To live and live and feign content,
Have beauty on face, weep may inside,
Await the moment I finally make peace,
Will begin my struggle free immortal life,
In life, no one ever lives his own life !!

Addicted To Poetry

An art, be it acquired or simply hereditary,
Putting vivid thoughts into exquisite words,
Magician's tricky stick, poet's addiction is poetry;
Cultivated experiences of heartfelt sweet weirds,
Music of life, unsung songs,
skill of warriors' swords !

Trust Me

Dejected in love
I act in defiance of,
Yet face the music
Why not look into my face,
Embrace panoptic passion !

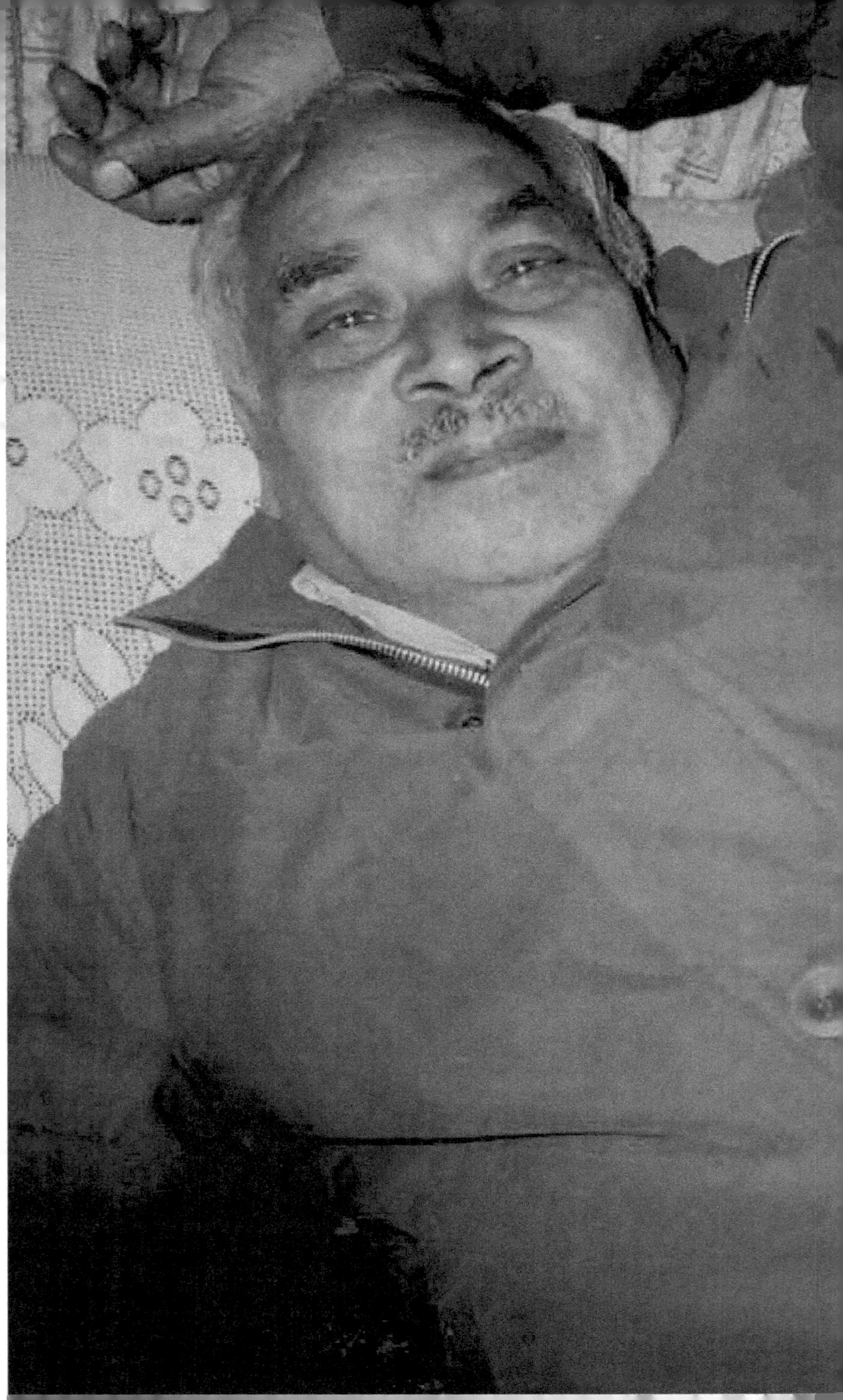

Happy Birthday Dad

Ever since you left us all in tears,
our hearts ached in grief for years.

Sweet memories of times together,
brush gently as subtle touch of feather !

Longing to touch you and embrace,
while feeling your presence at every place.

Your smiling face in my eyes I embellish,
but wonder why in a blink you vanish?

That in my each cell you are very much alive,
It was too late to realise and end up strife.

Remember the days of joy, None of them so sad,
Today I am wishing you happy birthday dear Dad!

Antiques

Romans and Greeks
Sound synonymous to antiques,
Symbols of Renaissance
Old yet fashionable,
Not bygone are the most valuable;

Classical stamps of the aeon
Singing chronicles of yesteryears,
Resurging and Reawakening past
Are the antiques!

Precious history coming alive
Culture visible a priceless scribe,
Massive learning for the present
Since what are known present today,
Will be memorable antiques of tomorrow !

A Spring Day

I reply to the song of cuckoo, my favourite bird,
Sun shines brilliant and then clouds take their turn,
Blossoms at trees carpet as breeze swiftly stirred,
Cheerful chase of butterflies
ends on evening return,
A spring day rescues all from a summer burn !

Trees leaves and grass all go intense in green,
Promising for youth to retrieve optimistic room,
Chirpy birds float and fly and reattain their sheen,
Passion of first love that eats up all the gloom,
A Spring day even can turn cacti bloom !

Heart To Brain

Thinking you do and send me commands,
Muscular I can pump to the whole
Without a single miss day through night,
Why should I ever listen to you,
When might is always right !

Whispers Of Love

Neither in a reclusive nor in restricted,
Close to the wind, whispers of love sail,
For want of a dialect with the beloved,
Impatient soul feeds on the holy grail !

His every look deep into my eyes,
Takes my breath, I heave a sigh,
Drumming beats echo heart to heart,
A music subtle yet melts the stars !

I find my soul dook in moonlight ,
Vivid thoughts put up a constant fight,
Create an aura around that enraptures,
Whispers of love go beyond capture !!

Moonlight

A white coat in my courtyard at night,
As quiet as the shine of the fresh snow,
Moon reverberates but sun's luminous light,
A smuggler's enemy is silvery moonlight !

A gleaming sparkle on a dreaming face,
Reaching for the moon and getting over,
Drilling deep into sea, turning noctilucine,
A perception that it's a moonlight !

Good Karma

*Through successive phases
of our existence
Traverse our deeds,
And the salvation by
deeds becomes destiny,*

*Deliverance of mankind
Is the karma,
Ploughing the soul
Beautiful or ugly,
Retributive justice done
Through and through,*

Morals and ethics
Obedience and respect,
Honesty and staunch
Righteous living, dedication,
The good karma !

Frees of all desires
Hence all sufferings,
Hence reincarnation,
Final destination
Meeting the absolute,
Through good karma !

Entwined

In pure love entwined
the knittings of a mother,
Through icy cold winds
embrace child's subtle being,
As warmth shows on rosy cheeks.

Living In Present

Bygone is past, memories echo,
No one can live in antiquity,
There's no time like the present,
Future comes apace, an opaque mirror,
Live a life of endeavor, live to your full,
Till the air is able to fill !

Achievements, the jewels of past,
Present is the very life of life,
Why ponder over future, unknown pal,
Also when it comes soon enough,
Live present moments in happiness,
A water that ought to flood !

First Date

Enamoured in love
Throbbing in solicitude,
My heart
I had already lost,
You were calm
as the eyes spoke,
Love tugged at
heartstrings,
Melody rhymed and
flowers blossomed;

Essence of infatuation
turned true,
As fresh as
a morning dew,
As bright as
twinkle of stars,
Emotions flowed
to beyond words,
My first date
My Prince Charming !

Hello January

Eleven months is too long a wait to greet,
Hello January ! At last you are here,
I was zealous to receive you this new year!

Some shiny pearls of intense merriment,
Amused throughout the year and gave a blow,
Let fill your heart and the face glow!

Some new resolutions to be made with you,
Few unkept promises solid as a bundle of water,
Must be kept and shared with you !

Some missing strands of mission unaccomplished,
Still ought to be executed this month,
Anticipate an appreciation from you!

Few events the source of unhappiness,
Though seem difficult to be forgotten,
Let them die earlier to you!

Hello! A brand new January,
You are getting younger year by year,
I yearn for a close encounter with you!!

The Ordinary Mug

Coffee mug, mediocre and customary,
Though a marvel of paint and pottery,
Rests on a levelled shelf of kitchen,
Peeps out of glass anxiously.

I pick up every fine morning,
So that it doesn't go uninspired,
To make a great shake of coffee,
Of no unexceptional ability.

Quenches intellectual thirst,
That invokes impulses most unusual,
Starts the day with a bang,
Making the maximum and the most anyone could.

No lesser than a reverend it behaves,
Extraordinary mission by the ordinary,
Atonement of the satiety with pleasure,
Returns to its jurisdiction the glass shelf !

Smoke

Smoke emanating from heart,
Stirring ideas sprout in brain,
Giving flush to my face...

Path is scary,
Heart pounces to protrude out
of the breast bone,
Legs shake in trepidation...

I am awake with heavy eyelids,
With hope that glitters
in my eyes,
And arms await a tight
embrace...

Candles glow in pitch dark,
Only bright spots
that enlighten,
Moments of togetherness...

You tune up to my delight,
addicted to me, a surprise,
Smoke engulfs
To nobody's sight...

Desires

Deep rooted longings in the heart,
Emphatic and obdurate in temper,
Salubriously nurture the imperial thoughts,
Intripid expressions are bound to stay,
Realistic approach will shape them true,
Endless efforts await in optimism,
Solace to desires abode is inevitable !

Bruzo My Dog

Little pup at my paternal uncle's house,
Moved from his mother's lap and chose mine,
Pure black, on forehead a white stripe,
Tears of love in his eyes, that I did wipe ,

Reached my home and added onto family,
Dear he soon became, grew up hastily,
Faithful, wagging his tail in affection,
Clever and alert, wit in perfection,

A burglar's alarm, awake at nights,
Sweet morning walks and evening fights,
Winters, summers, autumn, rains and fog,
With every season bloomed, Bruzo my dear dog!

Language of love unsaid, yet perfectly understood,
Pets are the best friends beyond any brotherhood !

My Garden

A heart full of passion,
Enchanting thoughts youthful,
My most beautiful garden !

Hundreds of buds blossom,
Red, yellow, pink, lavender,
Colourful flowers smile!

Fragrance in the breeze,
Melodious song of birds,
Dance of butterflies !

Greenery all over,
Differently designed grass,
Perfectly fashionable!

Morning sunshine,
Twilight of dusk and dawn,
Hues of optimism !

Currents of waterfall ,
Musical constant flow,
Never in reverse!

Garden is vast,
Take tireless walk
To the wholesome!

Sometimes it's autumn,
Flowers wither and leaves fall,
Endure, have patience,
Spring is sure to return
To my beautiful garden!

Why expect one colour?
Happiness,
Embrace all, sadness and distress,
It's a state of mind !

Why walk down one single path?
Comfort,
Explore the rest, struggle ,
It's a solace to mind!

Why have only one design?
Money,
Conceive others too, content,
It's an ecstatic unwind !

Heart never will lose passion,
Overflows the brimming mind,
My Beautiful garden !

Fragmant Of The Soul

A mighty unpleasant zephyr,
Slivered my soul into fragments,
And blew away my most valuable fraction.

Macrocosm became his hostelery,
Having gained altruistic radiance,
His silence became my tribulation.

Snookered by lot of malarkey,
Hoveled in dismay and haggling for aquittance,
I died a silent death every moment.

Now that time promulgates my totality,
As I rediscover that fragment of my soul,
My mind rests in serenity and content.

Just as I regain my thunder,
And manage to rise in bravado,
To live a life that I would evince,
Now a denizen of desires and aspirations!

Colour Blindness

Showcase of my favourite painted collection,
Piled up for years, eventually being inaugurated,
Without fail, what if colours were amalgamated ?
No one could ever unveil my apprehension,
Heart pouncing, breaths endured expansion,
More and more to the colours as I concentrated,
My senses shivered and swiftly hibernated;

My passion, my hobby could not be my profession !
Neutral to doctor's innocuous advice on colour,
Who proved out the reception on retina as deficient,
Creator himself had prejudiced me in chromacy,
Dreams of painting vibrant having lost all valour,
As literary gained power, hues became munificent,
Enriched in colors, now is a pen's supremacy !